Previews

Previews

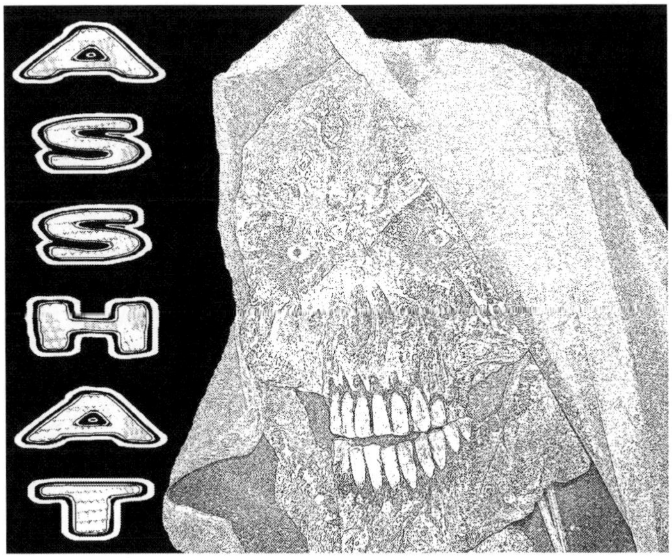

Previews

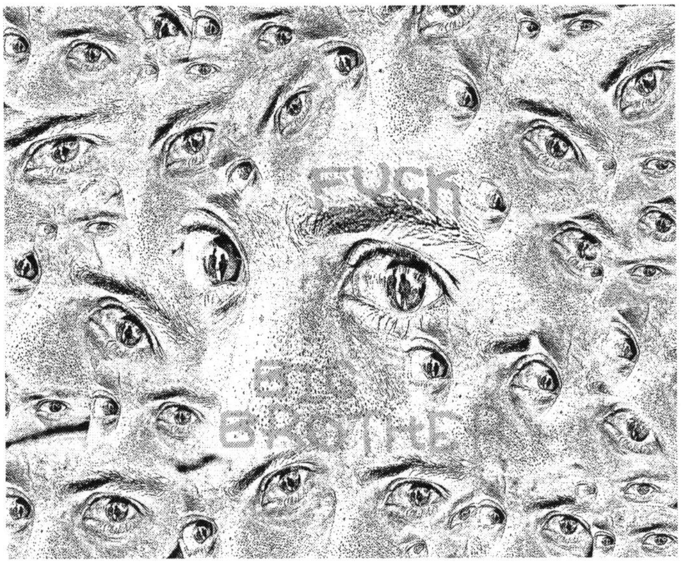

Previews

Previews

Previews

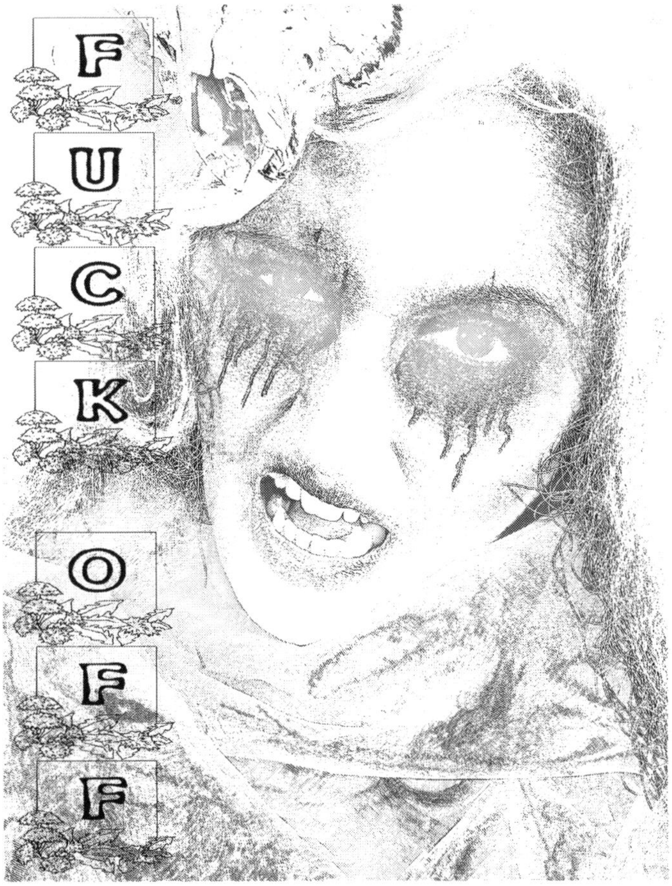

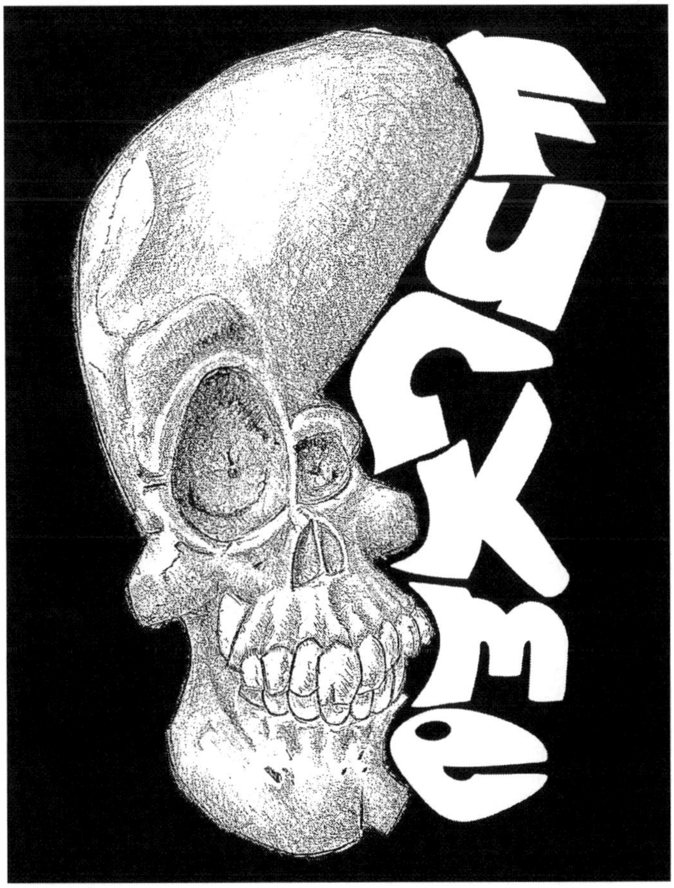

FUCK
THAT

FUCK YOU

EAT SHIT
AND DIE

ASSHOLE

BITE ME

PHILLIP RYAN.
ALSO WILLIAM RYAN.
ALSO DENIS RYAN.
PHILLIP (BARNEY) RYAN
BETTY MARGARET RYAN

SHUT THE FUCK UP

COCKSUCKER

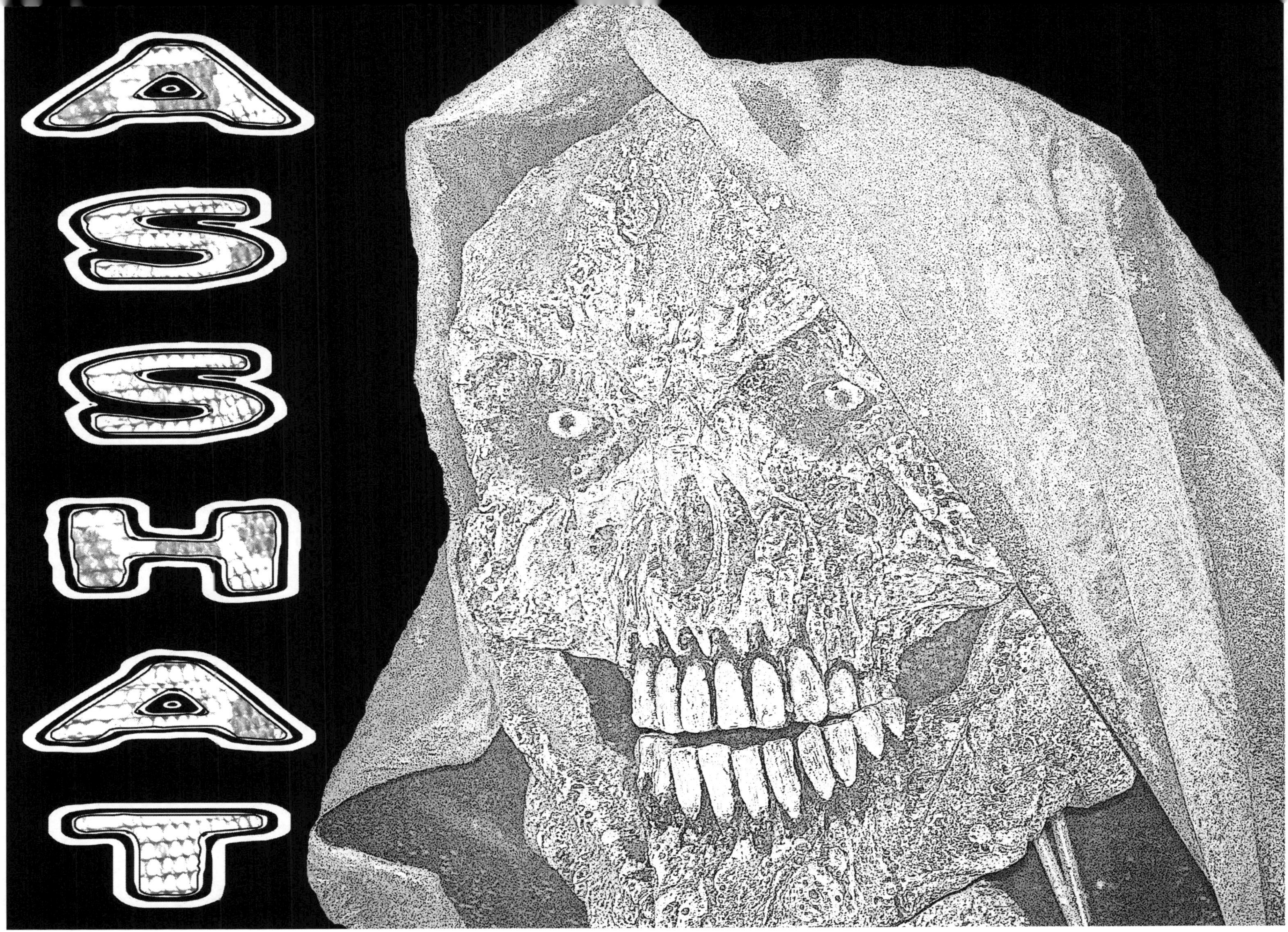
ASSHAT

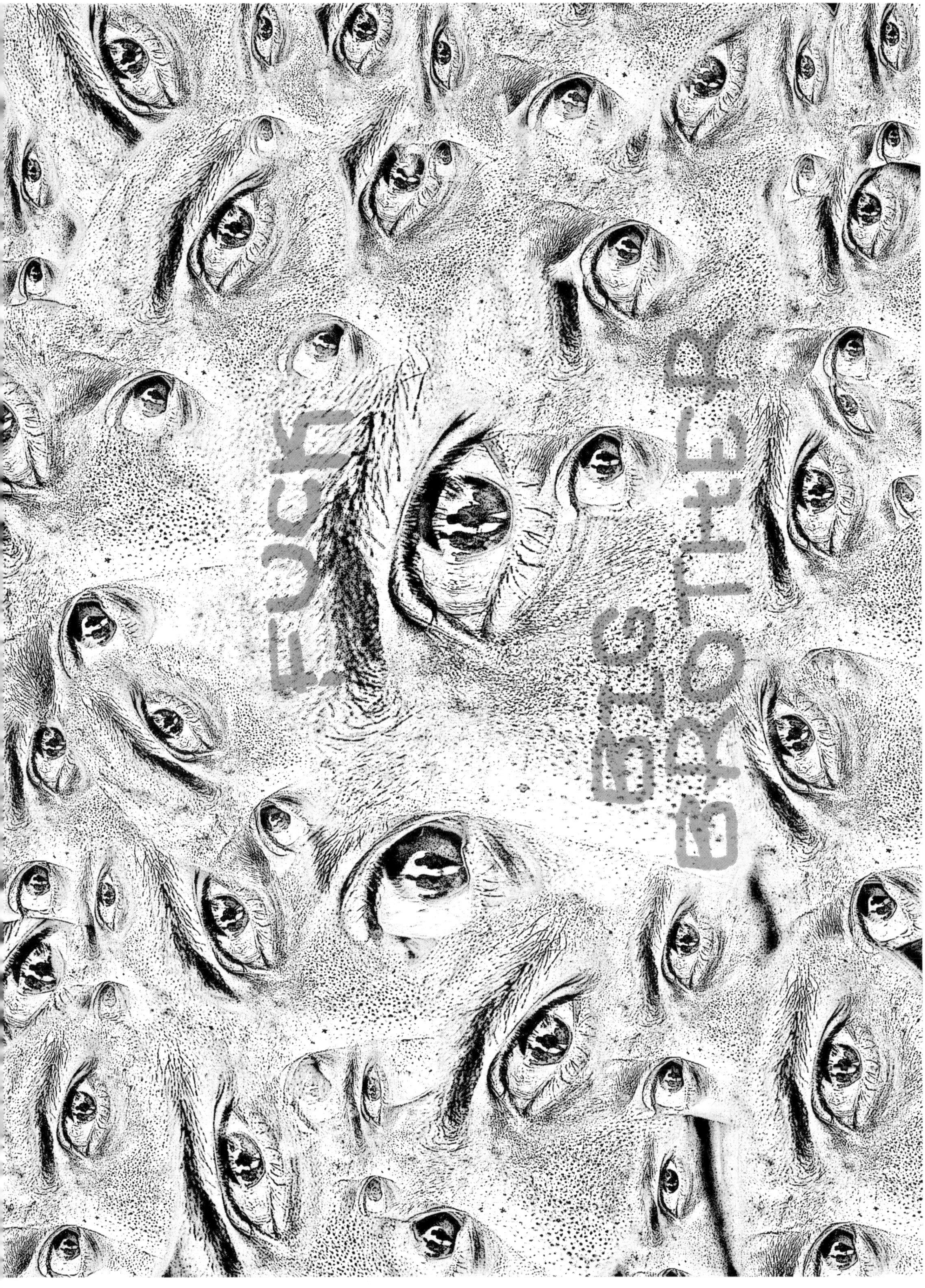
FUCK
BIG
BROTHER

wanker

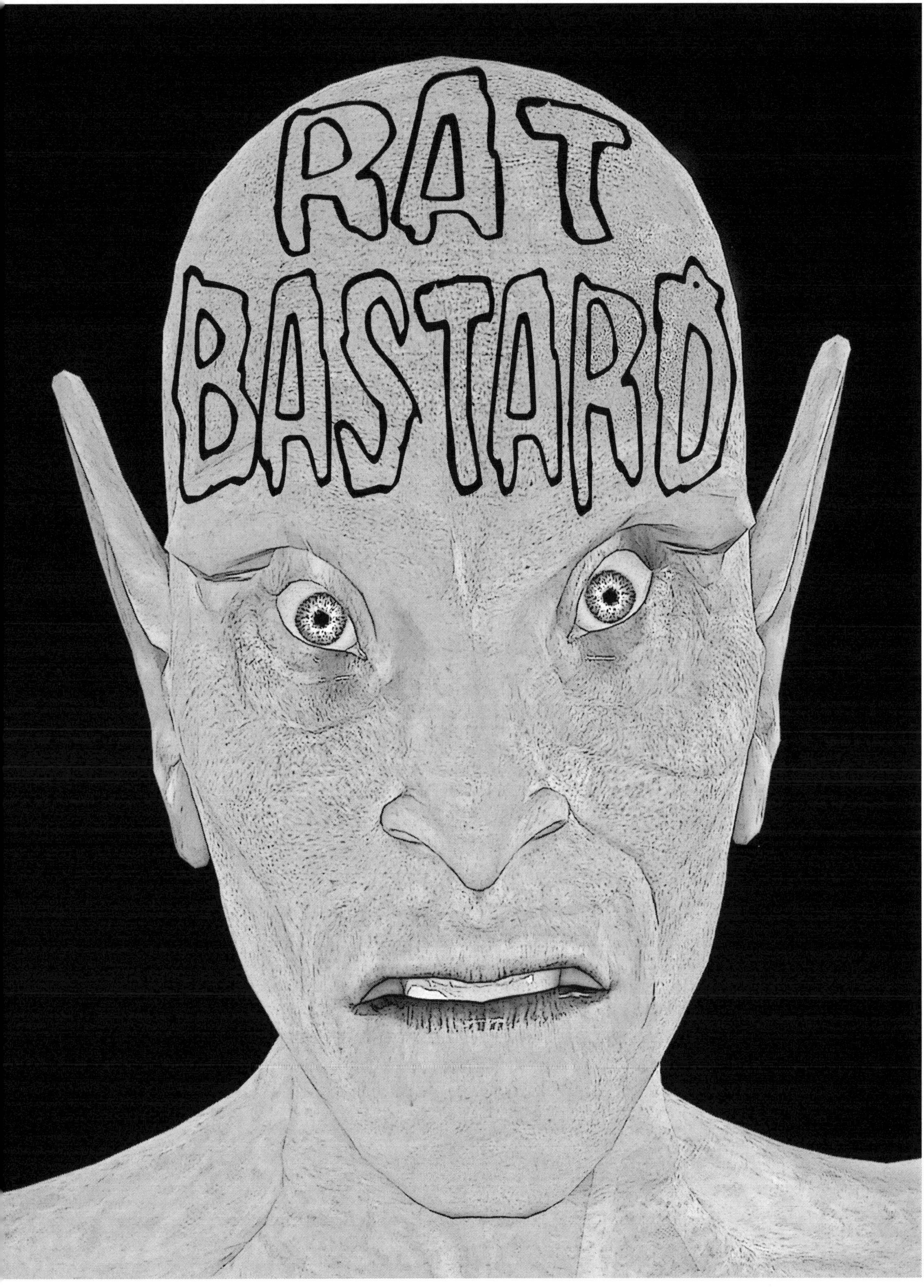
RAT
BASTARD

douchebag

BULLSHIT

CALM THE
FUCK
DOWN

BITCH

ass Face

PSYCHO
BITCH

give me a
fucking
break

BITCH FROM HELL

EAT ME

F
U
C
K
O
F
F

GO FUCK YOURSELF

FUCK ME

Color Test Page

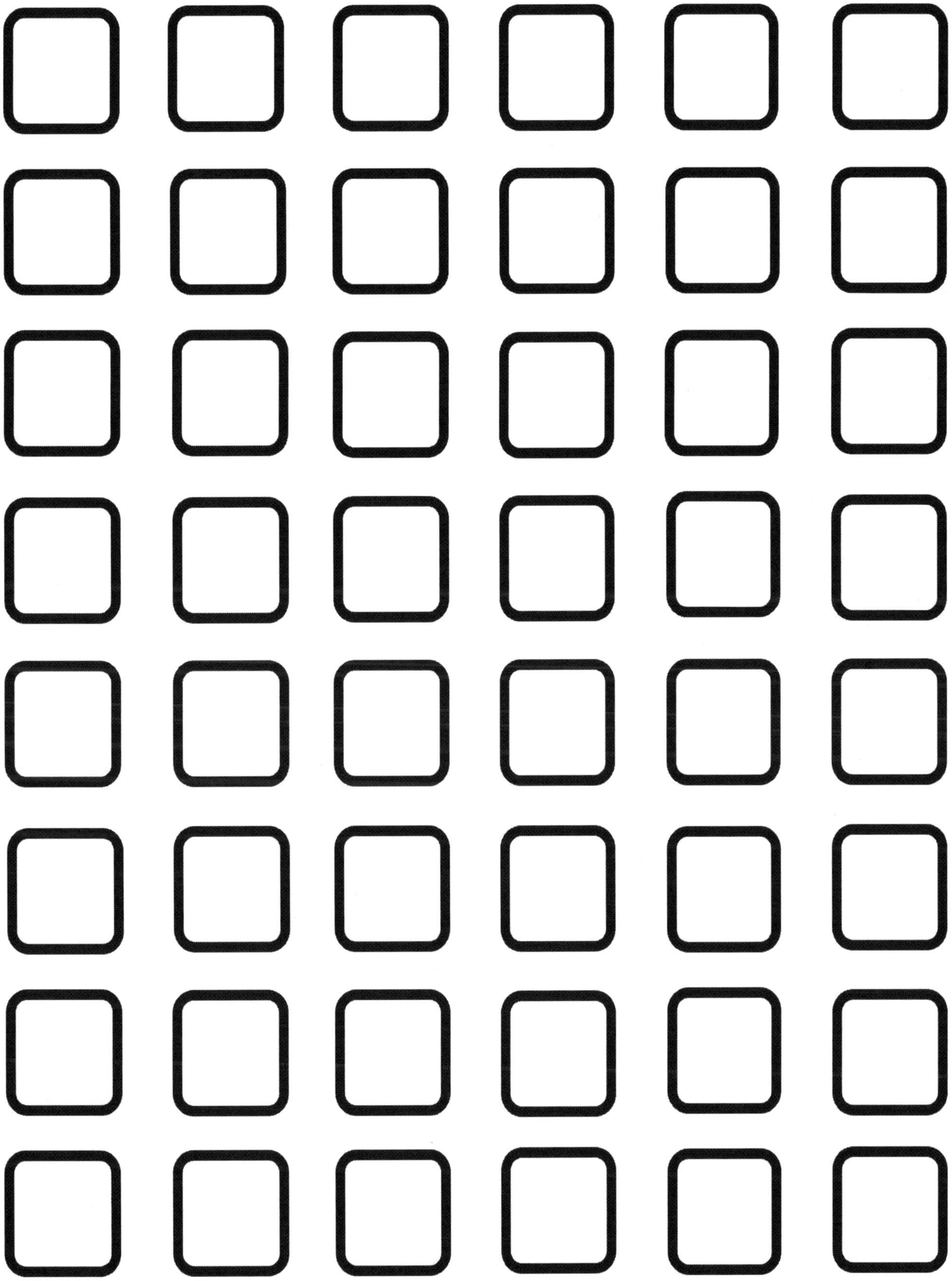

Color Test Page

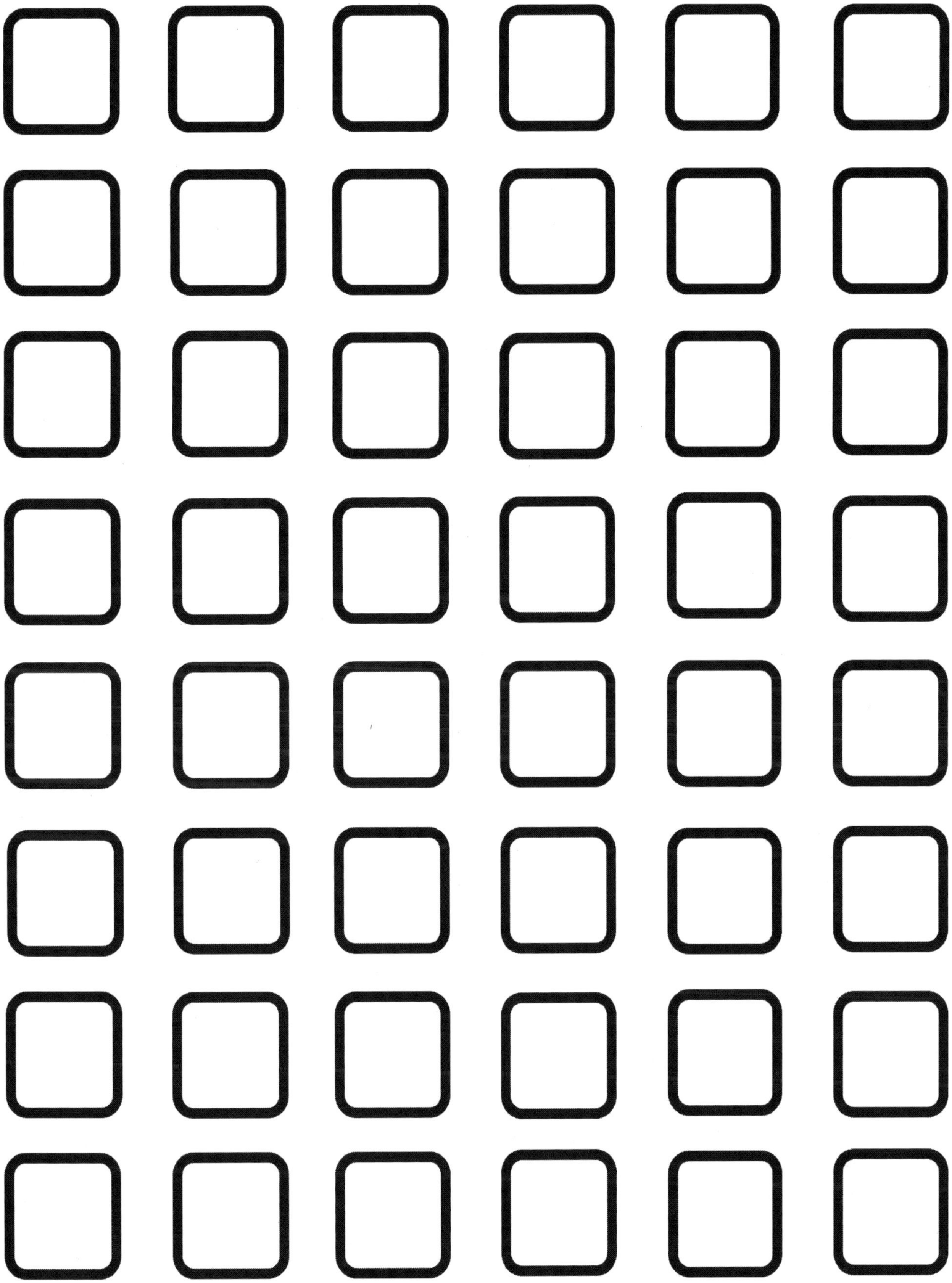

Made in the USA
Middletown, DE
10 December 2021

55133425R00044